I0426686

Terrorist This

by

James G. Garrison

COPYRIGHT 2006

ISBN 1-4116-6865-0

Published by LULU

TERRORIST THIS

BY

Dr. James G. Garrison

"All men.... are endowed…with certain unalienable rights. Among these **LIFE, LIBERTY…**"

Dedication

To all my patients, especially the Gulf War Veterans, who convinced me of the need.

Introduction

"From my angle I could only see a little of what they did. First kicking the crutches from under the man with one leg, then dumping someone from a wheelchair, then knocking down a pregnant woman and kicking her repeatedly in her abdomen, then…then…came the screams!"

"TWENTY NINE ROUNDS. That's all I had for the little .38. If they decided to overrun us would I actually get to fire them all? Would I go down fighting? Would I save one for me? If so which one? TWENTY NINE ROUNDS"

The flashback broke me from my shocked state. I likely would have been frozen there until it was too late if it hadn't! I quickly found out the back way was not nearly as secure as they must have thought.

No guards!!! Didn't want to miss out on the "fun", no doubt. After I felt I was clear enough I began the great circle to come up to the vehicle I had left earlier so that it was between me and them. Managed to resist the urge to peel out, as it would draw attention. However a surreptitiously raised finger and a muttered "Terrorist This", gave me enormous satisfaction.

The time and education since then has given me much reflection on those events. Why do we become unable to act when we most need to? Why do our instincts tell us to do things that are counter to what we should? Why did I use the grammatically incorrect terrorist instead of terrorize? **Why do they do these inhumane things to begin with????**

Once I had the answers how do I apply the knowledge in a manner that will be useful?

The mission became to write the definitive book on surviving terrorism, and then take a scissors to it. The people who should read this don't have time for a lengthy tome, won't remember surveys and studies, and are only confused by technical jargon. Larger print and fewer pages make for easier reading. Simple, short and to the point works! This is also your first lesson. Don't make your situation overly complicated. Assess your situation, apply the tips and relax. Excessive stress often is one's undoing. Calm and confident is the ticket to safety

CONTENTS

Chapter16

Home at Last

Chapter 1
Rules for the Captive

Rule 1:   SURVIVE

Rule 2:   SURVIVE

Rule 3:   See rules 1 and 2

It doesn't get any more basic than this. Dignity and pride and much more were left behind when you were taken. Your whole ego, most of everything you think you are, must be tucked away to be brought out another day. Seeing that there is another day is your only mission.

My first task is to scare you. Why? Because fear is your introduction to captivity. Mind numbing fear. Quickly followed by disorientation. Society's current obsession with political correctness and "feelings" has heightened our subjectivity to emotions. When we are confronted with total loss of liberty and maybe our lives it won't fit into the prevailing paradigm. All mental power is diverted to orienting; depriving us of critical thinking at the time it is needed most.

How bad will it get? Worse than you could ever imagine! Degradation and depravation make for a compliant and cooperative prisoner. Since Abu Graib forced nudity and sexual humiliation have become very popular coercions. Torture or mutilation may be done just for sport. Yes, I said mutilation. Few come out whole either mentally or physically, or both.

Pitting prisoner against prisoner is one of the oldest and most effective methods of breaking the will.

One of my early patients was seduced by the cheap novel's romanticized image of a mercenary. As a teenager he briefly fought in one of Africa's innumerable wars. His twenty man unit plus sixty conscripted locals were to hold one side of the village while the main force of government regulars swept in from the other. The conscripts, wanting nothing to do with this in the first place, broke and ran at the first shots. With this change in numbers most of the insurgents were able to escape. The regular's commander was furious. First he threatened to kill everyone, even those that hadn't run. But when five errant conscripts were rounded up he offered a test of loyalty. If the hired soldiers would execute the "deserters" they would be forgiven. Killing in battle is very different from murdering, but what choice did they have? Though they had their FAL rifles, the regulars vastly outnumbered them and possessed two heavy machine guns mounted on Land Cruisers. Fortunately their lieutenant stepped forward. The command would be carried out but only he would do the shooting. Whereupon he carefully placed one shot in the head of each to grant a quick and relatively painless death. The soldiers were spared both their lives and the guilt.

Like that lieutenant you must be prepared to mitigate the losses. It could indeed come to killing that more may live.

AND IT GETS WORSE!!!!

Now go back and read this from the start.

Next read it again.

When you have finished this book read it again.

Each time you confront a fear (any fear) you weaken it. Remember the saying "familiarity breeds contempt". Read, feel and confront until you have enough "contempt" that you will be able to think logically when the time arrives. This will give you an advantage over the captor. Maybe your greatest.

Chapter 2
What Kind of Captive Are You?

There are four basic types
Personal
Impersonal
Incidental
Institutional

Personal, obviously, means that they know your name. They will accept no substitutes. You and only you have what they want or have the importance to facilitate what they want. Usually this is the common kidnapping for money.

Only a few people or even only one may be involved.

This is the only kind for which resistance may be wise. Weapons will rarely be used on you for fear of "damaging the merchandise". However if you miss judge what kind it is there will be no "mulligan" or redo.

At this initial stage if you can raise an alarm or delay long enough they may defer to another day or another target. Even if you are taken you still have that advantage in escape attempts.

It should be noted that in some counties this has become a cottage industry. A person of means (to a poor peasant that is just about any westerner) finds a family member or valued employee kidnapped, treated well and quickly and safely returned. Abductors may actually apologize for the inconvenience. The ransom is always small enough that there is no difficulty in raising it immediately. Victims are commonly returned within 24 hours. Police are best not notified until after the return. Victims should resist the urge to raise masks or see the captors, since that changes you from a commodity to a witness. This gentile crime can turn ugly indeed when they perceive you as a threat.

The typical western kidnapping is a far nastier picture. Use as much resistance as possible. Remember, when fighting, that you have only a 1 in 5 chance of living if you are removed from the scene. Police should become involved at the first hint of a crime. The outcome will rely entirely on the competence of the authorities.

This category includes those that are taken for their knowledge, such as pass codes (dealt with in a later chapter).

Impersonal is like generic brands. An American, any Jew, any Muslim, a woman, a child, you get the idea. This is the most dangerous of all! Any problems and they will simply substitute another. A shoot at everything and take what survives attitude may prevail.

Incidental is the old "wrong place at the wrong time". A crime plan goes sour and you are the most convenient way to keep the police at bay.

Institutional is simply human pawns in a gigantic chess game. Agencies so nebulous they are unable to see you as a person rely on the effects on those who do. No one is so lowly as to be "under the radar" to them.

A possible **fifth** classification would be "free-ranging", people who are allowed to move about in public, but are bound by real or perceived threats. Cult members and battered spouses are amongst this category. Many volumes have been written on this subject so I won't go too deep into it here. The key to remember is not your captor's willingness to carry out the threat, but their ability to. A domestic violence complaint, in most jurisdictions, requires an automatic arrest of the party accused. A cry of Rape" in a public place will bring assistance immediately. Either case will bring you to the attention of the authorities to whom you may state your case. Even if a criminal action is not pursued you will be given ample time to contact any number of agencies that can provide safe haven.

Chapter 3
Personal

This heinous crime may be committed for the most noble of reasons; love. Male as well as female may be victims. The perpetrator's ego says this is the only way that they can be together as they are meant to be. Or it may say that it is too late and punishment must be delivered for failing to recognize "your destiny".

Keep your cool. Don't call him crazy, pervert or any of the colorful expletives that your naughtier side may have learned. In all captive situations angry outbursts only provoke angry outbursts and you are not in the best of positions to begin with.

It's time to see if that psych class you slept through seeped in a little. Discover the delusion then reverse it. You didn't reject him, he rejected you. You made the overtures and he didn't respond. Now you are the one who is mad and want to punish him but he has made this situation so we can never get this straightened out.

If you are convincing enough he will try to undo everything and see if you really mean it. When he starts to change plans resist the urge to make a break at the first opportunity. The longer you play the part the greater the control you have. Theoretically he could be persuaded to not only release you but surrender himself. At the minimum it should gain you better conditions and most importantly time. Time for others to come to your rescue.

Chapter 4
Impersonal

This is in many ways similar to personal except that you are merely a body filling in a concept of a person. You must first discover what this preconception is. Learning this is a very touchy situation. Conversation tends to disturb prejudices. If you do have the opportunity, begin to establish a rapport. Agree that he is right but that it is not you (the concept persona). You were forced by the greater evil (insert C.I.A., the current President or whatever you think he hates the most). "The enemy of my enemy is my friend" changes many an opinion.

If the concept is of a specific person, proceed as if it is a personal abduction and you are that person.

If communication is impossible a totally docile attitude is best. They expect, like Newton's law, every action shall have a reaction. Inflicting pain without the victim indicating misery delivers no gratification.

A well known terrorist organization had a history of taking captives to a particular courtyard and forcing them to kneeling position before execution. The pleas for mercy, crying and begging evoked a frenzy culminating in gunfire.

A group of Americans were taken to the courtyard.

No one cried.

No one begged.

No one died.

Deny the reaction and the action becomes meaningless.

Chapter 5

Incidental

You are in the bank on your lunch hour, cashing a rebate check for you forget what, when suddenly there are these men in ski masks. Explaining why you will be late back to work is now the least of your worries. Even with your face to the floor you notice the flashing lights appearing outside. The good guys and the bad guys are about to square off and you a smack between them.

In the introduction I stated that excessive stress is often one's undoing. Nowhere is this truer. The offenders are panicky because their "perfect" plan went sour and don't know what to do. The police outside are on an adrenalin rush and feeling the need to act violently to relieve it. When things get hot be the cooler. Once you establish yourself as such you become the last in jeopardy because you now have the greatest value.

Speak in slow, precise, clear and especially respectful tones.

Ask permission before any action. Don't look at them until allowed to.

"Sir. Sir." To the captors.

"May I comfort the woman that is crying?"

"Sir. Sir. If I close the curtains they won't be able to get a shot at you." Move slowly with hands held high so the authorities can identify you as a prisoner not a perpetrator. Now you have both sides considering you as not a threat. Continue in this vane. Be sure to tend to the other prisoner's needs less they perceive you as "one of them" which will greatly complicate the situation. Get coffee. Offer to deliver demands or bring in whatever they request from the negotiator. Resist the urge to "make a break for it", as the other prisoners will suffer for it.

Tell them your first name. Talk a little about your family. If it should come to executing prisoners to force demands it is far easier to kill a stranger than someone you know.

Don't get your hopes too high for a peaceful settlement. Ego tends to overpower the logic of surrender. And those that do these things have hyper inflated egos.

When the assault occurs, everyone with a gun will be shooting at anything that moves. **So don't move!** Face on the floor with hands on your head makes you a non-target. Don't even move or cry out if stepped on or else someone's reflex may turn deadly.

Chapter 6

Institutional

No one is so lowly or so geographically isolated that they can't become prey for a ruthless bureaucracy. It may not even be a glamorous international conflict but an agency turf battle such as I.R.S. or one of a zillion other agencies both home and abroad.

Two things are important. One: the more uncomfortable your confinement the more pressure is put on whoever their real target is. Two: you are totally at the mercy of others to resolve the issue.

Given this you must immediately turn all your attention to the details of your new environment.

Begin With the full cooperation with your immediate supervision. They see this as just another job and will make it very unpleasant for you if you make them more work or problems.

When introduced into the general population of the institution, realize that things are now at the most primal. A pecking order has already been established and you are an interloper. A person that looks and acts like they are important and powerful is more likely to attract the attention of those that actually are. Know what value you can be. Do you have contacts that can move messages outside?

Are you trained in law or something they find useful? Master chef? Entertainer? If you have nothing then you are only good for elevating the position of others and that is a very bad place to be.

Chapter 7
Captive comfort

Comfort is a test of will between you and your abductors. They want you miserable to break your will, make you compliant. You want to feel good so that you can concentrate on what to do about your confinement. Your first rule is "wet cold – dry warm". Water wicks away body heat 25 times as fast as air. Keep away from drips or puddles in your area. If necessary, create a slightly raised platform of debris or even dirt to stay on. Use anything dry to stuff your clothes or cover yourself. I have many times used crumpled newspaper or magazines to survive a night. Cardboard can be fashioned into an amazingly warm blanket. Dried grass or straw, around the world, has stuffed more mattresses than foam rubber!

Conversely, a water soaked bandana tied on the head is the field workers air conditioning. Water soaked clothes are even better. In a building that I needed to work in, I kicked out an air vent near the floor and opened an upper window, thus creating a convection air current. By hanging a burlap bag over the vent with the end soaking in a pan of water, the temperature dropped 15 degrees in a 20 x 50 room.

Water for these purposes can be obtained from nearly any source even if polluted. Even urine is acceptable although it leaves an odorous residue.

Chapter 8
Health and Hygiene

Keeping healthy has to be your first priority. You can accomplish nothing unless your body and mind are up to it. Cleanliness takes on new meaning. Washing yourself and your only clothes regularly keeps your spirits up as well as fighting infections. Pound the end of a stick to make a tooth brush. Splinters can become tooth picks. Even a corner of a cloth rubbed across the teeth will avoid the buildup of plaque… Salt makes a very good toothpaste and disinfectant. If you can get your captors to provide a little with your meals count yourself fortunate. Salt in scratches and open wounds is painful but amazingly effective at preventing the blood poisoning that leads to amputation or even death. Salt has been the standard treatment for whipping victims for centuries.

Avoid the urge to hide in a dark corner. Insects like dark corners and will enjoy your body heat and flesh if given the chance.

Silver is extremely useful, and I don't mean just as decoration or currency. Before refrigeration it was standard practice to drop a silver coin in a container of milk to retard spoilage. Silversmiths discovered the water used to quench the hot metal had remarkable curative powers. The first antibiotic approved by the FDA was colloidal silver. Colloidal is produced by running an electrical current between two silver electrodes suspended in water. The water is then drunk. Silver held against a wound will keep it free of infection. A coin under the tongue treats sore throats. Heating a coin in a fire then dropping it in a cup of water increases the potency. A few dimes hidden under the insoles in shoes will increase the chances of your survival. It will reduce your foot odor as well. It is best to avoid the modern laminated coins as they are contaminated with other metals that are harmful. Warning! The FDA approval was later withdrawn over the side effects. Silver sometimes causes Argyria if exposed to too much ultra violet. Argyria is a condition that can turn the skin gray and hard like slate. Also kidney damage can occur if the suspensions are over three microns in size. And every dose causes gastro-intestinal distress due to the elimination of the bacteria necessary for digestion. Acceptable for emergency situations but don't use if conventional medicine is available.

Open wounds must be closed by any means possible; sewing, duct tape, paper clips or clamps, even staples or pins. If infected permit flies to land and lay their eggs. The larva (maggots), have eaten away many a gangrene before it spread. Leaches are even better but likely won't be available.

Burning the wound with a hot iron is effective at sealing off bleeding. The scar can always be repaired when you regain your freedom.

Running your fingers through your hair is helpful if you don't have a comb. The combing action maintains the insulating properties of your hair while checking for parasites that might have moved in. Good grooming raises your spirits and defies your captors.

Clean drinking water is often a problem. Dysentery from bad water is very unpleasant. It is doubtful that you will be permitted a fire to boil water but that is best when available. A crude filter can be fashioned from a handkerchief or bandana fastened flat to a makeshift frame. Spread a thin layer of sand or crushed charcoal on it and pour the water on top and catch it as it trickles out below. Repeat several times. If you have more cloth available more layers increase the efficiency. Bandanas are fantastically useful tools and you should carry one or more at all times.

Chapter 9

Exercise

Keeping your muscles flexible and ready for whatever comes is important as well as good for keeping your spirits up.

Any exercise that you do is better than none. Use whatever is available. There are famous newsreels of a man on death row using his cell bars for a stair stepper and upper bunk for a chinning bar.

What is your favorite form of exercise? (I don't mean that which is normally done in a bed!!) What you do on a regular basis for physical fitness. Do as close to that as you can invent. Even if you are bound flex your muscles as if you were doing it.

Decades ago experiments were done on frogs with one leg restrained. Electrical stimulation was applied equally to both legs. It was found that both the active and inactive legs developed similar muscle mass. Other experiments have found that merely thinking about the exercise for the same amount of time others actually did the exercise produced 30 to 50 percent of the muscle mass.

Chapter 10
MIND FLEXING

The mind demands to be occupied with something. If you don't turn it to useful things it will settle for destructive things, like fear. Keep it challenged. Use all your senses on your new environment. Can you hear vehicles outside? How far? Can you feel air movement? What are all the different smells?

Avoid getting lost in non relevant memories. It diverts you from the task at hand!

When faced with long stretches of boredom recite math tables or other procedures that you have previously memorized. By association with memorizing you stimulate your ability to memorize the minor details of your current situation. Minor details often are the most important!

If they are trying to get something out of your mind (such as passwords or lock combinations) you may decide to wipe that information so that they can never get it from you. You don't have to have the training of a double O spy to accomplish this.

To delete a number from your memory visualize it as on the wheels of a slot machine. Pull down the arm and only the last digit spins. Number sequences have a rhythm to them so always start with the last first. When the wheel stops it is a different number. Do this again and again until you no longer know what number was the first on the wheel. Continue the process with each of the other digits.

To overwrite text visualize it printed in front of you then begin substituting random words or phrases. "The truck convoy will go through *Mary had a little lamb.* The *lamb trucked* through the convoy. *Mary* will go through *the lamb* convoy." After enough times even pharmaceuticals will only get the nonsense.

Caution! This is so effective that no one (except this author) will be able to bring it back. Don't use until absolutely necessary.

Chapter 11

Dealing with other Captives

When your computer solves a problem it doesn't just look up the correct answer. It locates thousands of tiny bits of information and assembles the answer. Each captive will have a somewhat different experience with the captors. The more information that can combined the more likely that you can find out what they really want, what they planning and what their weaknesses are.

Begin by getting the trust of the others. Introduce yourself. Tell them how you got there. Engage in small talk. See that everyone has a task to do and make sure they do it. The task could be looking under a door to for movements and figuring out routines. Or listening at a vent and reporting every sound even the ones that don't make sense. Keeping them both mentally and physically active helps them and helping others has a way of always helping you. They also are unlikely to have learned all that you have by reading this book.

Do not divulge any information that your captors may want or that they may use against you. Planted informers are not unusual. More common are weakened prisoners that will gladly give away anything to gain even a little relief. In the outside world you likely know one or more that would do anything to you just to suck-up to the boss. It certainly won't be any better when the stakes are higher.

When making a move, the greater your numbers the greater the chance of success.

Chapter 12
Escape

In an old barn of the Circus Museum is one of the smallest but most important displays. It is a flea circus. It describes how the fleas were trained by putting them in a glass enclosure with a glass cover. Fleas are incredible jumpers and the natural response is to try to jump out. They jump and hit the glass lid, which they cannot see. After a few days the glass is removed. The fleas, tired of banging into the glass, no longer try to jump even though there now is nothing to stop them. Their will is broken so are easily trained for the amusement of their captors.

Fear is the glass cover you will face. It immobilizes nearly everyone at sometime. Your captor may create opportunities for you to try to escape, knowing that he already has that direction covered (bumping your head on the glass). Let him think he has succeeded in breaking you. The sooner he thinks you are docile the sooner he will ease his guard.

A famous escape artist once said he "could escape from anything but the grave". A few have tried that too. If he can get in you can get out. Just keep trying.

Doors that swing out can be forced open. Doors that swing in expose their hinges. Why worry about a lock when sliding the pins from the hinges is so easy?

A method of escape once tried and punished for is unlikely to need to be as well guarded afterward, he will think, thusly is a preferred choice.

Once outside the best way to get away is to look like you aren't getting away. Try to blend in as much as possible. Find clothing that doesn't stand out. The dirty and disheveled are normally overlooked as beneath one's level in most societies, so aren't scrutinized. A tired shuffle is less likely to draw attention than a quick pace.

Travel as if you belonged. Hugging walls or sticking to shadows will attract as much attention as walking down the middle of the highway.

Appear to have a mission. Push a cart, carry a parcel, jot on a clipboard.

All predators (2 or 4 legged) instinctively see a creature going away from them as prey to be chased down. If you must cross an area that you might be seen get as far as possible to one side first then cross at a diagonal.

Avoid straight lines as they make it too easy to predict where you are headed and may be intercepted.

Don't head in the obvious direction. The opposite of that direction is the second place they will look. If the place you must go is due north then proceed south east (or south west) for a while, then north and finally north west (or north east as the case may be).

Chapter 13

Combat

We can assume that you are not a trained fighter so fighting fair is out of the question. The first rule of the kind of fighting you must do is to have the willingness to do whatever is necessary. The novice will typically strike a medium power blow then step back to watch the results, as if waiting for approval of what they did. Sure way to get the crap beat out of you! When you strike it must be with everything that you can muster. Continue attacking until there is no question your opponent cannot continue.

Forget about what is sporting. Only the dirtiest blows and tricks will count. Kicking the groin, gouging the eyes and hitting the throat are good starts

Forget about even facing you opponent if possible. Sneaking up on or blind siding is exceedingly wise.

A garrote may be fashioned out of any sturdy cloth, cord or, better yet, wire. Get a firm grip on both ends and cross your arms to form a two to three foot loop. Quickly drop it over the head of whoever making sure that it lands at the neck not the chin. Uncross your arms, put your knee in his back and pull for all you are worth! Don't stop until several seconds after he has stopped moving.

Anything that can be sharpened will give you an edge (pardon the pun). Plastic toothbrushes and turkey bones have made many a prison "shank". The more times it is stuck in them the more likely it is they will stay down.

What do you call the man who brings a gun to a knife fight: **a winner!** Always try to have a nastier weapon than those you face.

If possible get a little familiarity with guns before you get in these situations. Grabbing an AK-47 and not being able to get the safety off could ruin your day.

If you have read this far and still saying I couldn't do that, then don't. The opposition will not have the same feelings for you. Violence always brings an end, his or yours. If you can't finish it don't be stupid enough to start it.

Chapter 14
Torture

Torture is divided up into two groups, physical and mental. The reasons for torture, though, are a myriad.

You may be tortured for information. You may be tortured to gain compliance. You may be tortured because he had a bad day and wants to take it out on someone. You may be tortured because he had a good day and enjoys doing it. You may be tortured for reasons you will never know.

I would encourage the reader to seek out a competent Doctor of Hypnotherapy to learn pain control techniques. The same ones that ease dentistry can conquer physical torture.

If you have not yet seen the Doctor just pick a spot to stare at that is a little above eye level and a bit difficult to see. Count backwards from ten. Tell yourself that with each number you force the other numbers from your mind and your eyes grow heavier. By the time you reach five all the numbers will be gone and your eyes will be unable to stay open. With your eyes closed imagine you are at the dark top of a stairs that lead down to a very bright and beautiful place. Make the stairs as long or short as you need to feel comfortable and proceed slowly down, counting each step. When you take the last step off the stairs find yourself in the happiest place you could ever imagine! When your mind is in that place nothing bothers you. The body is hurting? Ohw well!

Another is moving the pain around.

With a very little practice this is possible. If you wish you may use the above technique by substituting a place where you have this ability for the happy place. First move it an inch to one side of where everything is happening. Then back to where it started. Then several inches to one side

. Then back again. The to and fro action creates a momentum to help increase each following move. Then you move it to the other side of the body. Then back. Soon this is so much fun you start wanting more just to have more to move around. People have been known to laugh and giggle when they should be screaming.

Psychological torture is a bit more complex. The key is the phrase "A tactic known is a tactic blown". By figuring out what is trying to be accomplished you will have the antidote.

The first stage will be fatigue the body, fatigue the mind or confusion.

Depriving of sleep fatigues the body. There may be a constant bright light that you are not allowed to turn away from or they take you in for questioning every 45 minutes. To counter this keep repeating in your mind "Everything that would normally weaken me now strengthens me". With this conviction you will find the few minute breaks can string together to be quite adequate.

Fatiguing the mind is easy. We all probably have felt it with our everyday jobs. (You always knew the boss was just torturing you!) What ever you do to combat it at work, do to combat the torture. If you can't physically accomplish it then do it in your mind.

Confusion is when you really have to play games. Basic truths will be reversed or twisted. Three fingers held up they will insist are four. The HooRah cry will become YaHoo. Green lights are white etcetera.

To anyone who has successfully learned another language the solution is easy. Dealing with letters that look the same but sound different and putting adjectives after or before nouns requires two or more levels of thinking. Both realities are correct and are easy to remember if not mixed. You must learn your captor's reality but retain your original reality. Review both frequently to avoid confusing them. Of course don't let on to the captor or he will change to another and you will have to start all over again.

Chapter 15
End of the Game

The manure is about to hit the fan. Your captor has no more time to play with you. You must now make the decision whether to give what he wants and lose your future value, which could result in your death. Or deny it with finality, which will probably anger him enough to kill you (some choice!). Additionally, if you have used any of the information wiping techniques (chapter 10) you have the quandary of whether you still have enough to satisfy the demands. For a complex situation a simple criteria is best: **"Will it cost Lives?"** Money or property can be replaced. Propaganda is as valuable as yesterday's news. Passwords and plans are usually changed as soon as it is known that someone who has access had been compromised. Surrendering such information, at the very least, should buy you some time as he checks it out.

Authorities may be waiting for him to do just that. A tiny portion of even the worst human has an urge to honor the bargain and let you live. Better yet, when he gets what he wants, he will not want to be bothered with coming back to deal with you.

Remember what you learned in chapter 1!!!

On the other hand, personnel movements, maps, diagrams, etcetera all indicate future activity that is quite likely to result in loss of lives. Furthermore, it is probable that you will be considered a liability that could interfere with the plans. Why not have the satisfaction of thwarting his plot when you have nothing to loose?

All this should be thought out and a decision made before this moment arrives. At the point of death few will be able to think clearly.

When you have done whatever you decided it is now time to practice disassociation. Battered children instinctively do this. Move your mind, you soul, to another place, away from your body. What happens to your body now feels as if it were happening to someone else far, far away. Ironically this may save your life. Ask any EMT about how many times it was not the wound but shock that kills. By relaxing the body it may be possible to avoid that fatal system overload. And how stupid you would feel if he didn't shoot you and you died of fright instead!

Chapter 16
Home at last

You made it! Maybe there was a great welcoming party, yellow ribbons and all! Maybe only the relief of being in your own bed, surrounded by your own "safe" things. Now for the good news-bad news. The good news is that you will be able to put it "almost" completely behind you. The bad news is that it will have to wait a while. This is not the time to forget but remember. Remember everything that you can. The authorities will want to debrief you (probably several times). You may have trial to testify at or an identification of your captor (remember when seeing him get his was what kept you going!). Most importantly the effort to recall all will give you an action, a direction to go. Doing something, anything, is critical right now. You are more vulnerable now than when were in captivity. First your normal world was taken from you then the artificial world. Now you are like an animal take from a zoo and released into the jungle, forced to forage on your own. Not knowing boundaries anymore. Only by understanding how you got to where you are can you know what direction to take next.

See to your health at one. The faster you finish any dental or reconstructive surgery the faster the physical reminders will be out of sight. A lot of exercise, healthy food and general R+R will be reassurance that you can deal with anything. In this case anyway, you need to fix your body before you can fix your mind.

Write everything down. Write a book. Wouldn't a best seller be poetic justice? Your children and further descendents should know what you had to overcome. Even an unpublished journal will give you a perspective in future years. "I wonder who this happened to. It couldn't have been me. I can't see how anyone could go through that and still arrive at the wonderful life that I now have."

This is when the healing really begins. The more that you think of this as a book the more your mind separates it from you. Put all your pain and anger into the book, and leave it there! Don't let it come back to you. It must stay in the book. It belongs there! Soon you will see your life as a timeline. From the day you were born up to "the book" and after "the book" until now. Concentrate on making the timeline "scar over" and become continuous again. "The book" will drift off to another reality, away from you.

A couple of tricks will help you control the drift. First make sure you have put everything in the book. This means all the personal "too horrible to deal with" things. Don't leave any roots from which the weed may re-grow. Next, in your mind, change it to a dreary black and white image. Research has shown that even so-called "color blind" see their world with some color. Removing all color makes it very difficult for anyone to relate to as being real. Removing sound is even better. The most dramatic subtitled old silent movie is seen as humorous by today's standard. Last, but not least, step away from the screen. The smaller the image the further removed it is from you. This is where the "almost" I mentioned at start of this chapter comes in. It is quite possible to use the shrinking picture to completely remove "the book (meaning the incident)" from your mind. Resist the temptation to do so. What has happened, now that you are in control of it, should always be part of you. It made you what you are proud to be today!